I F♥rgive MYSELF

CAST THE 1ST STONE

ERIC AND TAMAR GOODSON

Praise for *I Forgive Myself*

Eric and Tamar are truly the light of God in the earth. They go about being the helping hands and feet of Jesus to everyone they meet, and I thank God for their lives. They love so well, and they see everyone they meet through the eyes of God. When I sit with them, the heart and love of God towards me is what I feel, and I become so aware in those moments of how much I matter to God. They are precious gems of God and I love them so much.

—Tanya Walker, minister
Certified Coach, Teacher, and Speaker
with the John Maxwell Team

Love it! Your love is magical and is inclusive. It invites everyone in instead of excluding anyone. I love that about you guys! Magical! Makes me happy to be around you. You acknowledge those who have contributed to your growth and I am so grateful for the privilege of being in your lives. You have enriched me more than you can ever know. Your selfless contributions to the community are epic and your loving family. I love you! You have brought me so much pride in you and for you! Thank you for the wonderful honor! My cup runneth over. Love great!

—Susan Montez, LMSW
Actor, play director, Master of
Social Work (directed FACES theater group).

Eric and Tamar are phenomenal power couple and reflect the goodness of God in the way they love people. Their faith is contagious and ignites tremendous hope in hearts. Their down to earth approach and sound wisdom are an immense blessing to me. One of the most valuable attributes they possess is that they are relational and intentional with their connection. It is nice to be able to see that in the era we live in.

—Elisha Lloyd
Real Estate Agent
Toronto, Canada

Copyright © 2021 by Eric and Tamar Goodson

All rights reserved.

No part of this book may be reproduced in any form or by any electronic or mechanical means, including information storage and retrieval systems, without written permission from the author, except for the use of brief quotations in a book review.

All personal or group study is permitted and encouraged. Permission will be granted upon request. Unless otherwise identified, Scripture quotations are from the King James Bible®, ©Copyright The Lockman Foundation 1960, 1962, 1963, 1968, 1971, 1972, 1973, 1975, 1977. Scripture quotations marked (TLB) are taken from The Living Bible copyright © 1971. Used by permission of Tyndale House Publishers, Inc., Carol Stream, Illinois 60188. All rights reserved.

ISBN: 978-1-7373240-0-3

Cover design by Tommy Z Media,
https://tommyzmedia.com/

Interior design: Deborah Perdue,
https://illuminationgraphics.com/

Editor: Margaret A. Harrell, https://margaretharrell.com

Published by

LEGACY
EMPOWERMENT

Dedication

To our dads, who are no longer with us physically.

Foreword

What an adventure awaits your heart as you begin to read this book. As I read through the pages, it was as if the pages were reading me, highlighting different moments in my life. I begin to reflect and Ponder on each aspect of my life. This book will take you through a variety of emotions and at the end of that Journey your life will be brighter, and your heart will experience the comfort of God for yourself and others.

Somehow the authors of this book were able to go into different areas of my heart chamber, freeing up any wrong ways of thinking about others and myself. This book carries the transformative power of God's heart for you. It allows you to see yourself with great care and gentleness and it allows you to see yourself as a target for God's goodness and restoration. I'm so grateful that Eric and Tamar Goodson wrote This Book. I know it will touch many lives and bring people to a place where they forgive themselves, forgive others, and begin to live again. Instead of just trying to survive, they will be brought into Life by reading this book.

Amber Twigg

Pastor and founder of A. Twigg Ministries

Introduction

*P*erhaps you have been holding yourself hostage for months. Maybe even years, like many of us. Regardless of how long, any amount of time is too long to NOT forgive yourself.

I Forgive Myself is a revelation everyone can use for themselves. Often, we hear people say, "I forgive you," meaning that person is willing to let another person off the hook for whatever way the other person transgressed against them. Have you ever taken the time to really do some self-evaluation or feel within yourself that maybe, just maybe, you may need to extend the same grace towards yourself?

I Forgive Myself is a journey you will take to reflect on times when you should have, could have, and may now need to, liberate your own soul through self-forgiveness.

This is a journey of self-care, introspection, reflection, and conscious mental evaluation. It is time to show yourself kindness and some well-needed self-care by forgiving yourself.

Is this a selfish act?
Should I wait until whomever I have wronged, violated, messed up with, etc., extends grace and forgiveness to me before I can forgive myself?

The answer is simply—NO!

You do not need permission from anyone to forgive yourself. In fact, it's difficult to expect something from someone else when you have not first done it yourself.

I Forgive Myself is a very vital process that will help you value yourself and gain the confidence you need to move forward in your life without external validation or approval. Many of us have been starving all our lives, waiting for the forgiveness from others we deserve. We have received God's forgiveness, which is written in His Word. However, we often give others the power to hold us in bondage as we wait for their forgiveness.

I Forgive Myself will guide you in how to incorporate this ongoing practice as part of your being, understanding that your life depends on it. Your emotional stability depends on it. Your happiness can't exist without it.

For you to be all you can be and to live life passionately free, self-forgiveness is crucial. Some people, "holier than thou"—you know the type—consider themselves good, 100 percent perfect. They have nothing to forgive themselves for. I would say any such person is in BIG trouble and doesn't even know it. When you do come into the consciousness and realization that you are not able to cast the first stone, when your hands aren't as clean as you think they are, this book will be right here to see you through.

WE ALL MAKE MISTAKES—when Sorry is not good enough.

I have made so many mistakes. I have hurt so many people unintentionally. Most of my mistakes came from real estate transactions, early on. To start a business and lead *while learning* the business became more challenging than I anticipated. Let me say that despite the few bad experiences, there were certainly many victories. Over the long run, I have helped many people. So many other transactions were successful, and to date, wonderful relationships are still going strong.

But let's go back to when I was just starting out. Issues would arrive. People often wanted me to provide solutions, and the truth is—I was just learning to sort my way out, just like everyone else.

However, I had a leadership role, and that means I was required to take extreme ownership and responsibility on every single level. My role was real estate investor, in each of those transaction. My "investors" were inexperienced—never true investors. They were family, friends, or church members (we call each other brother and sisters). That was where my mistakes lay. They had no concept of expectations in such a business: you win some, lose some. As of 2020, I began a new process. I started a training program to first certify my investors before they can begin investing. This, I believe, will provide clear boundaries and expectations.

When to walk away

Here is what I learned. When your *sorry* is not good enough, do not lay your life down to be trampled on. Simply move on. No one can cast the first stone. Do not let shame take your voice. Do not let condemnation by way of unforgiveness rob you of moving forward.

CHAPTER 1

Self-Care Now

It seems as a society we have now recognized the importance of self-care. Whether it's taking a hot bath, sweating off stress at the gym, or taking time to meditate and pray, it's important we prioritize taking "care" of ourselves. In a busy world, with family, work, and millions of distractions, if we aren't setting aside time and space to care for ourselves, we will be eaten alive and be very unhappy people *very* quickly.

A less popular (but probably more important) form of caring for oneself is taking responsibility for ourselves. This includes acknowledging and owning whatever bad circumstance we might find ourselves in.

It takes bravery to look at poor outcomes and admit, even to the smallest degree, where we could've done better. Surprisingly, when we get over the discomfort of owning a 1 percent contribution to someone else's 99 percent, we find ourselves incredibly empowered and in control.

Nevertheless, receive Papa God's love and forgiveness. Forgive yourself if you have not lived up to what you expected of yourself, or if you have done something or said something to violate someone.

Normally, the process of making mistakes, will continue if you are living on this earth. The art of forgiveness is a practice for us. It's like giving birth. It's not something you master once; each time you experience it, it will be different.

KEEPING your heart open will afford you a smoother transition.

WE KNOW from firsthand experience that forgiving is one of the hardest things to do. One of the most difficult things we had to endure and learn to forgive each other for in our marriage was infidelity/adultery. We learned to work forgiveness and its layers into our marriage.

Don't mistake forgiveness with being healed. When someone is hurt, the healing process may take longer than the person's willingness to forgive. Both parties need to then exercise patience, perseverance, and empathy towards each other. We found out through this horrific experience of infidelity that caused wounds in both of us. Both of us needed time to heal. Both of us needed time to forgive each other, and both of us needed time to forgive ourselves so that we could truly forgive each other.

WHAT'S THE RUSH?

EXTENDING that care towards ourselves and each other was so worth it. We encourage you, as you deal with those old wounds that may be triggered by anything at any time, to love unconditionally, to be patient and kind towards each other.

THIS REQUIRES THERE TO BE true repentance, of course—first and foremost. Do not be foolish. If someone shows no desire and/or takes no practical steps towards changing bad behaviors, then do what the movie says, "Get Out." Of course, seeking God in everything you do and allowing Him to direct your path is of the highest priority. He knows the hearts of all people and holds each destiny.

FOR US, we didn't end in divorce, which would have brought its own set of pain. Instead, we decided to work through to the root of the betrayal, which began our healing process. So many times, due to lack of good counsel, people are under the notion that just because you forgive, you no longer hurt. That is a boldface lie! We must be patient with each other. Only God can heal wounded hearts and those memories that try to plague your mind.

DADDY ISSUES

CHECK this out—both of us had Daddy issues! Both of our fathers neglected and abandoned us in some fashion. It was inevitable that we would experience each other's outbursts of pain, anger, or rage. We both demonstrated these things differently.

We both needed to see God work through us. It is only when we did our work that God could repair the Daddy issues in our heart. And we both needed to find God's loving touch as we persevered, forgave, and served each other as our crazy worlds collided.

BEFORE YOU CAN HAVE a successful marriage, you must have the collision.

IN JULY 2020, I, Tamar, had to bury my father. I had to bury a father I had had little to do with and lacked a close relationship with. Through our marriage, I cried some sleepless nights upon the chest of my husband because I yearned for a dad who would demonstrate that type of father-daughter relationship.

Somewhere along the line, I was to be blamed for not trying harder or giving enough money to attain that demonstrative love from my dad. You see, my dad lived in Jamaica. My stepmom and sister took me from my dad when I was probably six or seven years old. I had only seen my dad one time, when I was about eight years old, before I migrated to the United States. Since I had made it to America and have made some sort of progress in life, the expectation was that I needed to help my dad, which I did, but always felt a bit of guilt for not doing more. I went back to Jamaica when I was twenty-two years old and saw my dad again. The first time since I saw him at age eight. I was so excited to see him but became instantly disappointed again because he left the same day. Just as I handed him what I had brought for him from America.

He left me again or to me at least that is how I felt. Regardless of feeling hurt again, over the years I kept in contact, sent money when asked, and yes, I did give money for quite a while grudgingly, but nevertheless I did. The last money I sent for my dad was Father's Day 2020. My father passed July 01, 2020. I allowed my hurt to cripple me from being transparent and asking my dad for what I wanted.

My father lived in poverty to the day he died, and I believe if I had been able to get the fact that my dad was not able to give me what I wanted, which was just love by way of reaching out to me, by way of phone call other than when there was a need—then I would have reached out more and been more willing to provide more financial assistance.

My truth, my dad had chosen another family. My older sister, ten years older than I am – became the parent of both of us. She was still underage herself. We were left to make it on our own. My stepmom, whom my dad was still married, to was now separated. My stepmom was in the United States but sent money back home to us in Jamaica, which provided us the luxury of boarding with family friends.

As I grew older. I poured my heart out to God. I slowly but surely learned to forgive my dad. My dad, I learned, was a quiet man. Having to bury him, I met so many of my cousins, uncles, and aunts, who I knew of but had lost contact with. They shared with me what a gentle, kind man he was. Many called him "Dad." As I reminisced on the time, he came to visit me around age eight—it was a beautiful, breezy morning. I woke early, as I always do. I was boarding with my uncle and his family, just a house next to where my family house still was, bolted up because no one lived there anymore. I sat on a little hill, playing with my stick dolls as the wind blew through my dolls' hair, I remember looking up, seeing in the distance my dad coming towards me. This was the most glorious day! It still is one of the best days of my life. I ran towards him and jumped into his arms. He twirled me around, and I felt the breeze going through my entire being.

I cannot help but imagine that my dad saw how happy I was and decided to leave me be, as he could not afford me that life where he lived. The area where I was liviing—it was a much safer area to live in. Where he lived was equivalent to the projects here in America. I was not able to perceive that until now. My dad, I believe, thought he was making the right decision by leaving me be. Now – I know it really was.

I love you, Dad. I miss you. May your soul rest in peace.

LIKEWISE, I (Eric) told my story to my wife about my broken relationship with my dad. One day I just allowed my heart to break. As a man it was extremely difficult to acknowledge the fact that I was hurting and wanted the love of my father. I wanted him to be here to teach me all the things about life. I was angry at him for his physical, mental, and emotional abuse of my mother, and for not trying harder to be my father, and for leaving the marriage, and for dying when I was fourteen years old. I needed him here now!

AS I ANGRILY SPOKE TO my wife about my dad, expressing my pain, hurt, anger, my wife began to share with me a different perspective that I had never seen before. My wife was able to ask a lot more questions than I could ever have asked my own mom over the years. I began to see my dad differently. Then I decided to forgive myself for choosing to hold on to the anger towards my dad; it totally liberated my soul. It was like the weight of the world was lifted off my chest.

THE TRUTH IS that it did not happen instantly, but as I began to have those quiet moments with Papa God, my heart began to open beyond my understanding. I hated my dad for an awfully long time because of how he treated my mom. It was not until I met my wife, who introduced me to, and demonstrated, such an unconditional love towards me and my father that that very unconditional love opened my heart to forgive my dad. This act of forgiveness renewed my mind to truly realize that I loved my dad and missed him dearly. I took a giant step and chose to forgive him, even though he is not physically here with us. I chose to fall in love with him all over again. I love you, Daddy.

CHAPTER 2

Hey, Dad

DADS NEED TO FORGIVE THEMSELVES TOO

Our Dads died with so much pain, shame, guilt, and the need for someone to extend forgiveness to them. There are so many homes of single-parent families. Usually the mom is the one who stays to take care of the kids when Daddy decides to leave the relationship and abandon his kid(s).

WE WANT to take this moment to give honor where honor is due. We want to honor all the fathers who have been there alongside their families, leading them, being a strong role model, tending to their garden, and building their legacy.

AS CHILDREN, we listened to our mother gingerly tell stories about our father. Over the years we watched her reminiscing, trying to camouflage her feelings of pain, hurt, abandonment, and shame. We even carried her pain, because we too suffered from the neglect, lack of presence, and abandonment from our father. As children, we only needed to hear our mother say, "I forgive you for all the wrong you have done to me, . forgive you for hurting me. I forgive you for not being there for our children. I forgive myself for holding on to the pain and sharing that pain with our children." Wow, what an amazing legacy to pass on to your children. A legacy of forgiveness.

JUST THAT ONE statement would have turned things around and empowered so many lives. Jesus demonstrated this act of forgiveness with the woman caught in adultery.

JESUS ASKED all the woman's accusers to cast the first stone, but could they?

IF WE COULD EXTEND this hope to our fathers, perhaps they will live longer, perhaps they will die in peace. Perhaps they would become better fathers.

NOTHING WE CAN DO WILL CHANGE the fact—they are our Fathers!

IF YOU ARE a dad who finds yourself in a position where you may be seeking forgiveness from your loved ones, you should know that it is not too late or too soon to forgive yourself. The reason you feel so much pain, guilt, shame, and remorse are because you have a deep desire to change but don't know where to start.

WHY DON'T you start right now by forgiving yourself?

DO NOT WAIT for the former spouses, ex-girlfriends, or baby mamas to extend forgiveness to you.

RIGHT NOW, if you desire to change and want to improve your contribution to the lives of your children and others you may have hurt, start here. Forgiving yourself doesn't mean others automatically just let you back in or will even choose to forgive you.

HOWEVER, when you accept the love God has for you, when you accept God's forgiveness, you then can forgive yourself. Forgiving yourself will cause you to behave in a manner that is more edifying to yourself and to those around you.

**PLEASE SAY this simple prayer
and believe in your heart:**

Father, forgive me. I am sorry. I love you. Thank You so much. I forgive myself for the things I have done. Now list the things you want to forgive yourself for below. When you are finished, receive that you have been forgiven yourself.

I Forgive Myself

Chapter 2 – Hey, Dad

CHAPTER 3

Mommas Aren't Perfect

Did you know your mother is not perfect? Moms are always there. Well, for the most part. We do want to acknowledge the moms who may not have been the typical nurturing mother. You also need to forgive yourself, as not being the typical Momma Bear.

FOR THE MOMMA Bear who has always been there: you have raised those children; you've sacrificed everything for your children. You may have worked several jobs, stayed in unhealthy relationships being a martyr for the cause of the kids to provide for your family.

NEVERTHELESS, you fell short and turned into a controlling, manipulative parent. You may not have spoken poorly of the children's father; however your nonverbal communication towards their father demonstrated to the children that he was less than a man.

WHAT YOU HAVE NOT REALIZED IS that no matter what relationship you have or had with the children's father, it is grossly inappropriate to share your bad experiences with the children, in a demeaning way, by belittling their father.

THE CHILDREN'S relationship is a child/parent relationship, and yours was a spousal relation- ship. Children often feel stuck, left to choose between parents. The truth is that most children care for and love both parents, no matter how poorly one of the parents behaves.

WHEN PARENTS DO NOT ALLOW children to freely have a relationship, from *their own perspective*, about each parent, a vicious cycle goes into effect and has anchored a bad behavior that causes pain for an exceptionally long time—if not forever.

Chapter 3 – Mommas Aren't Perfect

MOMMAS, this is an act you must forgive yourself for and correct the bad behavior. Free those babies, whether grown adults or young children. Forgive yourself for the part you played in why your marriage or relationship did not work.

FORGIVE yourself for staying too long in a relationship you knew was not healthy.

TAKE ownership for passing on toxicity to your children. When you forgive yourself, you are now free! You will no longer feel entitled and hold someone hostage. You are living your life and raising your children. The legacy you want to pass on is love, not bitterness.

Mommas aren't perfect, even though they might seem like they are Superwoman most times. The area they often fall short in is the area of forgiveness. Sacrificing so much to raise their children, it can happen that though they do not realize it, their hearts have become stone-cold towards others and themselves. Mom, you matter as well, and forgiving yourself is about self-care. Free yourself from what was, so that you can freely BE the helpmate that God created you to BE.

**PLEASE SAY this simple prayer
and believe in your heart:**

*PRAYER OF FORGIVENESS:
I am sorry, I forgive myself, I love myself—
Thank you*

List the behavior and/or things you have done to infringe upon your children and yourself:

If more paper is needed, feel free to grab some and continue this process.

_____

_____

_____

_____

_____

_____

_____

_____

_____

_____

_____

Chapter 3 – Mommas Aren't Perfect

Receive God's love because you have forgiven yourself!

CHAPTER 4

Siblings' Childhood Wounds

What do you remember about growing up? Was your house filled with laughter or pain? How many siblings do you have? Was your household a blended family?

THERE IS no doubt that there are beautiful memories we all try to hold onto, growing up. But we must not forget that there are also some negative childhood experiences we endured with our siblings that ingrained themselves into our hearts and minds, which played a major part in shaping us to be the way we are today.

MOST OF US, for the most part is carrying baggage from our childhood, holding something against our siblings for several different reasons.

Maybe it's because our brother or sister was more favored by one parent. Maybe it's because our siblings are from a blended family. Maybe it's because our siblings treated us badly. Whatever the cause, we've learned to hold grudges too close to our hearts. As adults, we can't seem to understand why we can't get along with our brother or sister.

LET'S do a quick exercise to scan our memory. I invite you to take a few deep breaths to settle down and close your eyes. We want you to go back to when you were between the ages of five and seventeen.

WHAT CAN you recall that made you mad/upset/angry that perhaps a sibling did to you?

HAVE you ever had one of your siblings be so mean as a child that as you got older, you held onto that hurt your brother or sister caused you? Perhaps they teased you about something or in another way treated you really badly.

THIS IS CONSIDERED SIBLING child wounds.

MOST FAMILIES LIVE with these experiences, and never talk about them. No wonder there is always some type of family feud, right?

I LOVE the story of Joseph in the Bible, and if you are not familiar with that story, it can be found beginning in Genesis, Chapter 37.

JOSEPH WAS betrayed by his own sibling and sold into slavery. Later in life, Joseph became powerful. He could have placed all his siblings in jail or even ordered them killed. But as we fast forward into the story, in the end Joseph did the right thing. What was the right thing?

THE RIGHT THING was to confront his brothers. I imagine Joseph had not spoken about his childhood wounds for years, and here he was, faced with his siblings. He could have remained unidentified and retaliated or simply just tucked the memory under the rug, like many of us might do. Many people would have taken revenge, but Joseph executed a care-frontation.

WHAT CAME out of Joseph's care-frontation was an amazing, beautiful family reunion. The forgiveness work had to be done, and it only took one brave step towards forgiveness.

IT IS imperative that you locate yourself in the dynamics of your childhood wounds and make a quality decision to be the initiator of forgiveness—forgive yourself, so you can forgive your siblings.

**PLEASE SAY this simple prayer
and believe in your heart:**

*PRAYER OF FORGIVENESS:
I am sorry. Please forgive me.
I love you.
Thank you.*

List the behavior and/or things you may have done to violate your siblings in any fashion or form. When you are complete, decide to take the initiative to ask for forgiveness from your brother or sister.

_____

_____

_____

_____

_____

_____

_____

_____

_____

_____

_____

_____

If you feel like you have exhaustively tried before, then receive your own forgiveness. Receive God's love, so that you know you are forgiven.

Poem

We want to take a break from the chapters to guide you through a healing process. This healing process is found within this dynamic poem. This is a self-forgiveness activation for you, so please read it out loud.

> I choose to forgive myself
>
> My heart is in unrest
>
> My tears caress
>
> The feeling of hopelessness
>
> If only you could just feel my pain
>
> I promise you I have nothing to gain
>
> Except to relieve this discomfort—I disdain
>
> I choose to forgive myself

I Forgive Myself

You may never forgive me

That is not the goal, you see

I forgive myself—If you can also find it within your heart, then forgive me

Know this—I forgive myself

I am no longer at your mercy

I am no longer tied to you to liberate me, affirm me, or release me

I forgive myself because God already did

CHAPTER 5

Leadership

Where do we begin? Our positions of leadership are sometimes assumed unintentionally. Then there are times where it's bestowed upon us. In other words, this is a legacy you must carry on. We will begin with the true story of Prince Harry, who renounced his legacy and leadership position to live a normal life.

The first question: is this guy crazy? Why would you do that?

PRINCE HARRY DECIDED that he did not want history to repeat itself. His mother, Diana, Princess of Wales, was killed in a car crash in a tunnel in France because the media was always after a story. Prince Harry was traumatized because he lost his mother. Along the way, he found his true match in Meghan Markle (an American), whom he married with hundreds of millions of people watching, broadcast on every television network and streaming platforms.

His wife was a famous TV actress who left Hollywood to marry Prince Harry. A year into their marriage, she developed severe depression and wanted to die. As a royal, she had lost all the independence she had taken for granted earlier. She did not like the new life, and she felt the British media attacked her relentlessly. In January 2020, Prince Harry made a leadership decision to lay his "Royal Highness" title (among others) down for his wife. He was attacked by the media. He decided to lead his family, sacrificing his position to show true love, and live a life as a prince, even thou he had no crown. That, my friend, is true leadership.

WHEN YOU WALK into a leadership position, your roles and responsibilities cause you to weigh heavily the consequences of your actions, and the effectiveness of your leadership.

Chapter 5 – Leadership

CAN you identify yourself as a leader?

ARE YOU A PARENT? Are you a teacher? Are you a doctor? Are you a lawyer, or are you a farmer? What is your leadership role?

HOW DO you live your life every day? How do you influence your home, your community, your school, your workplace, or your church? What part does that play in your life? Do you take orders or give directions? My point is, you are a leader in one way or another.

AS A LEADER, I know that my actions and how I lead affects the lives of others who depend on me. It is OK to show vulnerability. It is noble, to bring empowerment to those I lead and influence. I have a responsibility to treat the people I lead with honor. It is important to understand that when I make a mistake as a leader, I must not be too proud to say I am sorry but rather admit I was wrong. As a leader, you are expected to continue to self-develop, to be the best leader that you can possible can be.

PRAYER for those Leaders who feel they have fallen short as leaders:

Please forgive me, God, I have failed as a leader. I have caused so much pain, strife, and separation because of my position of leadership. I acknowledge my mistakes, stubbornness, pride that prevented me from changing, or even asking for help. I am sorry. God, help me. List the behavior and/or things you may have done to violate your position of leadership in any fashion or form. When you have finished, decide to take the initiative to ask for forgiveness from those you may have offended.

I Forgive Myself

Chapter 5 – Leadership

CHAPTER 6

Chains Are Broken

Sometimes we don't realize that we are still carrying the baggage of unforgiveness towards ourselves. Let me point out some scenarios and ideas that will help you to locate yourself.

HERE WE GO:

Can you talk about the former problem without getting an attitude or becoming defensive?

IF NOT, then there is more work for you to truly heal. The truth is, when most of us have this issue of forgiving ourselves, this is called a stronghold. That is a chain that needs to be broken. To start, accept the love and forgiveness of God. Then you will be able to move beyond the stronghold and forgive yourself. It may seem difficult, since those whom you may hurt and cause pain are unwilling to forgive you. Remember, you do not need the forgiveness of others to be free.

CHAINS ARE BROKEN when you choose to forgive yourself. Chains are broken when you receive the Love of God. Chains are broken you when you can acknowledge and accept that your actions have caused impact, negative effect on lives of others. You can sincerely and remorsefully express your apologies, allowing others the space time and process they need. Chains are broken then. Chains are broken out of that obedience when you step out and seek God for your healing through First Forgiving Yourself.

PRAYER:

I forgive myself for all the mistakes I have made and for all the things I have done that brought hurt and/or pain to anyone. God, I receive your Love and Grace. I receive that you have Forgiven Me. God, help me to Forgive Myself. I have no desire to keep going in a direction that does not serve me and that is causing others pain. List the behavior and/or things you may have done to violate anyone, in any fashion or form.

I Forgive Myself

Chapter 6 – Chains are Broken

Seven ways to practice the art of forgiveness.

1. Forgiveness statements – get a piece of paper or book and pen. Begin writing your statements. I forgive myself for and list what you are forgiving yourself about. Continue this process as many times as needed and for however long necessary. When you are complete. Burn it or shred it. You must let it go now.

2. Truth Journal – Be total honest with yourself in this journal. What have you learned from your mistakes? Every time, you feel yourself going back to a mistake you have made, begin my writing what you have leaned from it. Keep this journal and only write your truth in this journal.

3. Co create – be creative, do some artwork, make something. Draw a picture, take some

photos of nature or whatever interest you. Whatever art form emerges for you, do it. Energy cannot be destroyed only transferred. create something it will help you to release whatever energy you are feeling.

4. Be still – sometimes silence, quietness is the answer to your soul. Perhaps you just you can listen closely to what is going on inside more closely. Being still can facilitate grounding you. Precisely what you need to liberate your soul. Listen to your heart.

5. Tapping – explore tapping.

6. Affirmations – Write out three sentences today that will empower you. Repeat as many times as needed.

7. Meditate – Find whatever form of meditation that works for you.

CHAPTER 7

The Final Word on Forgiveness

I invite you to visit the scripture in Matthew 6:14. This scripture reads in the King James version:

"FOR IF YE forgive men their trespasses, your heavenly Father will also forgive you: But if ye forgive not men their trespasses, neither will your Father forgive your trespasses".

THAT IS THE FINAL WORD.

This word applies to YOU. You must forgive yourself as well. It is none of your business anymore if someone chooses not to forgive you. Your work and faith are to believe first that when you ask for forgiveness, you will receive Forgiveness.

PRACTICE THIS EVERY DAY, and it will become easier for you to extend forgiveness to others, even when they have not asked for it. This new way of being will bring joy, peace, happiness, and rest to your life.

Chapter 7 – The Final Word on Forgiveness

My thoughts:

CHAPTER 8

Proven & Researched: Unforgiveness and Your Health

Unforgiveness is choosing to hold to hurt, betrayal, trust broken or emotional pain. Unforgiveness is the cause of many things including:

~ Cancer

~ Low self-esteem

~ Bitterness

~ High blood pressure

~ Heart disease

I know it's easier said than done, right. That is just the truth. However, you must realize that you are not hurting anyone as much as you are hurting yourself when you choose not to forgive.

How to learn to forgive:

It's your choice

The pain is even more intense when someone that is awfully close has hurt you. Yet still, it is a necessary step if you want to begin to heal.

Extreme Ownership is taking responsibility for the part you played and then some, which will make you a better leader.

Forgive yourself!

You will find the more you practice forgiving yourself, the easier it will become to release others and forgive them. How can you do for others when you do not do for yourself?

The first step towards healing is Awareness.

Check in with your emotions constantly. Be aware first and foremost about your emotions towards another—especially negative emotions such as jealousy, bitterness, or anger.

Acceptance

Isn't this a big one? Most times, we stay in a relationship because we cannot accept the facts. We disregard our experience or our truth. Forgiveness does not mean you necessarily you have to continue in the relationship. You accept the facts and experiences, and you courageously move on.

What did this experience teach me?

Be radically honest with yourself with this question. This is an inner work. It's your work.

Initiate a conversation.

Sometimes it is helpful to hear the point of view of other person, who hurt you—of course, if you can handle it. If you are not able to, then it's OK.

Conclude one way or another . . .

To move on in a healthy manner—here is a suggestion:
Write a letter to the offender, or if you are the offender, write a forgiveness letter to self.

The worst you can do is keep reliving that dreadful time. Keep replaying it over and over in your head. Keep asking yourself crazy questions, paraphrasing after paraphrasing—*What could I have done better?* I pray you see this. It's done and gone. The only thing now is to move on one way or another. This is the very reason—I forgive myself.

My thoughts:

My Thoughts:

Contact us:

www.LegacyPPA.com

Email: admin@legacy.com
Follow us on Facebook @

www.ingramcontent.com/pod-product-compliance
Lightning Source LLC
Chambersburg PA
CBHW071817160426
43209CB00003B/125